Table of Contents

Record of Scores—Book D (Unit 24) 3

Summative Test

Step 1: Phonemic Awareness and Phonics 4

Step 3: Vocabulary and Morphology 6

Step 4: Grammar and Usage 12

Step 6: Speaking and Writing 17

Progress Indicators

Test of Silent Word Reading Fluency (Form A) 18

DRP (Degrees of Reading Power) Reading Test (Form C/D-2) 21

Spelling Inventory 28

D1506720

SOPRIS WEST EDUCATIONAL SERVICES
A CAMBIUM LEARNING COMPANY

BOSTON, MA • NEW YORK, NY • LONGMONT, CO

Printed in the United States of America

Published and distributed by

SOPRIS
WEST
EDUCATIONAL SERVICES

4093 Specialty Place • Longmont, CO 80504 • (303) 651-2829
www.sopriswest.com

Student's Name: _____

Summative Test—Book D

Number Correct / Total # of items	Phonemic Awareness and Phonics	Vocabulary and Morphology			Grammar and Usage		
	Word Study	Section 1 Vocabulary	Section 2 Word Relationships	Section 3 Morphology	Section 1 Grammar	Section 2 Usage	Section 3 Sentence Structure
Number Correct / Total # of items	10	10	10	10	10	5	10
Percent Correct							

Step 6: Speaking and Writing

Composition Rating

Ideas and Development	_____
Organization	_____
Voice and Audience Awareness	_____
Word Choice	_____
Sentence Fluency	_____
Written Language Conventions	_____
Average Composition Rating	_____

Progress Indicators—Book D

	Test of Silent Word Reading Fluency Form A	DRP Reading Test Form C/D-2	Spelling Inventory
Raw Score	_____	_____	_____
DRP Unit Score		_____	
Grade Equivalent	_____	_____	

Summative Test

Step 1: Phonemic Awareness and Phonics
Word Study Part A

> Read the word in bold. Find another syllable that is the same type (e.g., closed, vowel digraph) as **rain**. Fill in the bubble for your answer.
>
> **Sample: rain**
> - Ⓐ beet
> - Ⓑ row
> - Ⓒ tane
> - Ⓓ con

Directions: Read each word in bold below. Find another syllable that is the same type as the syllable in bold. Fill in the bubble for your answer.

1. **loud.** Find another syllable that is the same type as **loud.**
   - Ⓐ load
   - Ⓑ pane
   - Ⓒ low
   - Ⓓ coin

2. **lee.** Find another syllable that is the same type as **lee.**
   - Ⓐ ler
   - Ⓑ tec
   - Ⓒ eye
   - Ⓓ bead

3. **gle.** Find another syllable that is the same type as **gle.**
   - Ⓐ gul
   - Ⓑ jil
   - Ⓒ ble
   - Ⓓ gol

4. **urn.** Find another syllable that is the same type as **urn.**
   - Ⓐ run
   - Ⓑ ral
   - Ⓒ ert
   - Ⓓ unt

5. **lock.** Find another syllable that is the same type as **lock.**
   - Ⓐ sole
   - Ⓑ kick
   - Ⓒ oint
   - Ⓓ out

Step 1: Phonemic Awareness and Phonics
Word Study Part B

> Read the sentence below. Identify the stressed syllable in the underlined word.
> Fill in the bubble for your answer.
>
> **Sample:** Malik completed his **project** on time. Which syllable is stressed
>   in **project**?
>
>   Ⓐ The first syllable is stressed.
>   Ⓑ The second syllable is stressed.
>   Ⓒ The syllables are equally stressed.
>   Ⓓ Neither is stressed.

Directions: Read each sentence below. Identify the stressed syllable in each underlined word. Fill in the bubble for your answer.

6. The movie was **projected** onto the screen. Which syllable is stressed in **projected**?
    Ⓐ The first syllable is stressed.
    Ⓑ The second syllable is stressed.
    Ⓒ The third syllable is stressed.
    Ⓓ The syllables are equally stressed.

7. We will **remain** in the stands until the end of the game. Which syllable is stressed in **remain**?
    Ⓐ The first syllable is stressed.
    Ⓑ The second syllable is stressed.
    Ⓒ The syllables are equally stressed.
    Ⓓ Neither is stressed.

8. Tim said, "Science is my favorite **subject**." Which syllable is stressed in **subject**?
    Ⓐ The first syllable is stressed.
    Ⓑ The second syllable is stressed.
    Ⓒ The syllables are equally stressed.
    Ⓓ Neither is stressed.

9. We were **disappointed** with the results of the test. Which syllable is stressed in **disappointed**?
    Ⓐ The first syllable is stressed.
    Ⓑ The second syllable is stressed.
    Ⓒ The third syllable is stressed.
    Ⓓ The syllables are equally stressed.

10. We will **assemble** the pieces of the puzzle. Which syllable is stressed in **assemble**?
    Ⓐ The first syllable is stressed.
    Ⓑ The second syllable is stressed.
    Ⓒ The third syllable is stressed.
    Ⓓ The syllables are equally stressed.

Summative Test

Step 3: Vocabulary and Morphology
Section 1—Vocabulary Part A

Read the sentence below. Select the correct meaning for the underlined phrase in the sentence and fill in the bubble for your answer.

Sample: We had to <u>take cover</u> during the storm.
- Ⓐ get a blanket
- Ⓑ seek shelter
- Ⓒ read a book
- Ⓓ hide

Directions: Read each of the sentences below and the possible meanings. Fill in the bubble for the answer that gives the correct meaning for the underlined word or phrase in each sentence.

11. Don't <u>waste your breath</u> with excuses.
- Ⓐ breathe harder
- Ⓑ useless talking
- Ⓒ lie
- Ⓓ promise

12. Our records <u>indicate</u> that you have a perfect safety record.
- Ⓐ ask
- Ⓑ wonder
- Ⓒ point out
- Ⓓ inquire

13. My sister is <u>annoyed</u> because her CD is scratched.
- Ⓐ gone
- Ⓑ aggravated
- Ⓒ shopping
- Ⓓ cheerful

14. I can't afford the <u>expense</u> of a car.
- Ⓐ cost
- Ⓑ fuel
- Ⓒ loan
- Ⓓ payment

15. The victim <u>cried out</u> for help, but no one heard him.
- Ⓐ sobbed
- Ⓑ whimpered
- Ⓒ shed tears
- Ⓓ shouted

Step 3: Vocabulary and Morphology
Section 1—Vocabulary Part B

Read the sentence below. Select the word that does NOT mean the same as the underlined word. Fill in the bubble for your answer.

Sample: My sister is very <u>clever</u>.
- Ⓐ smart
- Ⓑ skillful
- Ⓒ intelligent
- Ⓓ humble

Directions: Read each sentence below. Select the answer that does NOT mean the same as the underlined word. Fill in the bubble for your answer.

16. She <u>whispered</u> something under her breath.
- Ⓐ talked softly
- Ⓑ murmered
- Ⓒ spoke quietly
- Ⓓ listened carefully

17. Your room has been <u>tidy</u> for weeks!
- Ⓐ quiet
- Ⓑ clean
- Ⓒ orderly
- Ⓓ neat

18. We don't want to <u>waste</u> time collecting the duplicates.
- Ⓐ use up
- Ⓑ consume
- Ⓒ spend
- Ⓓ look up

19. I did a <u>fabulous</u> job on my final exam!
- Ⓐ adequate
- Ⓑ wonderful
- Ⓒ great
- Ⓓ amazing

20. Speeding is not <u>tolerated</u> in the parking lot.
- Ⓐ put up with
- Ⓑ recommended
- Ⓒ allowed
- Ⓓ permitted

Summative Test

Step 3: Vocabulary and Morphology
Section 2—Word Relationships Part A

> Read the word in bold below. Select a **synonym** for the word. Fill in the bubble for your answer.
>
> **Sample: clever**
> - Ⓐ smart
> - Ⓑ fast
> - Ⓒ popular
> - Ⓓ cute

Directions: Read each word in bold below. Select a **synonym** for the word. Fill in the bubble for your answer.

21. **inquire**
    - Ⓐ call
    - Ⓑ tell
    - Ⓒ ask
    - Ⓓ sing

22. **drowsy**
    - Ⓐ sleepy
    - Ⓑ hungry
    - Ⓒ ill
    - Ⓓ spoiled

23. **hinder**
    - Ⓐ behind
    - Ⓑ back
    - Ⓒ argue
    - Ⓓ prevent

24. **immense**
    - Ⓐ smart
    - Ⓑ power
    - Ⓒ enormous
    - Ⓓ size

25. **annoy**
    - Ⓐ bother
    - Ⓑ assist
    - Ⓒ spoil
    - Ⓓ support

Summative Test

Step 3: Vocabulary and Morphology
Section 2—Word Relationships Part B

Read the word in bold. Select an **antonym** for the word. Fill in the bubble for your answer.

Sample: preserve
- Ⓐ finish
- Ⓑ save
- Ⓒ destroy
- Ⓓ protect

Directions: Read each word in bold below. Select an **antonym** for the word. Fill in the bubble for your answer.

26. **integrate**
- Ⓐ combine
- Ⓑ separate
- Ⓒ mix
- Ⓓ subtract

27. **spontaneous**
- Ⓐ planned
- Ⓑ immediate
- Ⓒ impulsive
- Ⓓ planted

28. **formal**
- Ⓐ dressy
- Ⓑ informal
- Ⓒ shape
- Ⓓ royal

29. **temporary**
- Ⓐ timed
- Ⓑ short
- Ⓒ brief
- Ⓓ permanent

30. **often**
- Ⓐ delayed
- Ⓑ frequently
- Ⓒ seldom
- Ⓓ never

Step 3: Vocabulary and Morphology
Section 3—Morphology

Read the sentence below. Select the answer that will complete the sentence. Fill in the bubble for your answer.

Sample: A person who has lost all hope could be called _____.
- Ⓐ hopeful
- Ⓑ hoping
- Ⓒ hopely
- Ⓓ hopeless

Directions: Read the sentences and possible choices below. Decide which word or phrase completes each sentence. Fill in the bubble for your answer.

31. A person who drives a car could be called a _____.
    - Ⓐ motoring
    - Ⓑ motorist
    - Ⓒ motors
    - Ⓓ motor

32. When you take in a breath, you are _____.
    - Ⓐ exhaling
    - Ⓑ haling
    - Ⓒ inhaled
    - Ⓓ inhaling

33. When someone commits a crime, their actions are _____.
    - Ⓐ legal
    - Ⓑ legalize
    - Ⓒ illegal
    - Ⓓ illegally

Directions: Read the following sentences and select the word or phrase that answers each question. Fill in the bubble for your answer.

34. If the root **ject** means to throw, what does the word **ejected** mean in this sentence?

    The pilot was ejected from the cockpit as the plane crashed.
    - Ⓐ thrown in
    - Ⓑ thrown out
    - Ⓒ elected
    - Ⓓ dejected

35. If the root **tract** means to pull, what does the word **retracted** mean in this sentence?

The pilot retracted the wheels of the aircraft after take off.

Ⓐ lowered
Ⓑ moved
Ⓒ pulled back
Ⓓ flapped

Directions: Read the sentences in each item below. Select the word that will answer each question. Fill in the bubble for your answer.

36. The goods were **imported** from Italy. The word **imported** is derived from the Latin root **port**. What does **port** mean?
Ⓐ pull
Ⓑ carry
Ⓒ lift
Ⓓ drop

37. The weatherman **predicted** the storm two days ago. The word **predicted** contains the root **dict**. What does **dict** mean?
Ⓐ see
Ⓑ locate
Ⓒ label
Ⓓ tell

38. Which word is derived from the Latin root meaning **to lead**?
Ⓐ prospect
Ⓑ distract
Ⓒ conduct
Ⓓ effect

39. Which word is derived from the Latin root meaning **to throw**?
Ⓐ project
Ⓑ respond
Ⓒ respect
Ⓓ retract

40. The suffix **-ous** means **to be characterized by**. The team rested after a **rigorous** workout. What does rigorous mean?
Ⓐ harsh
Ⓑ easy
Ⓒ relaxed
Ⓓ cold

Summative Test

Step 4: Grammar and Usage
Section 1—Grammar Part A

Read the sentence below. Decide if the underlined word is an adjective, noun, preposition, or none of the above. Fill in the bubble for your answer.

Sample: There was an <u>enormous</u> mound of trash beside the road.
- (A) adjective
- (B) noun
- (C) preposition
- (D) none of the above

Directions: Read each sentence. Decide if the underlined word is an adjective, noun, preposition, or none of the above. Fill in the bubble for your answer.

41. The submarine cruised <u>beneath</u> the surface.
- (A) adjective
- (B) noun
- (C) preposition
- (D) none of the above

42. The <u>entertainment</u> was cut short by the power failure.
- (A) adjective
- (B) noun
- (C) preposition
- (D) none of the above

43. During the rainstorm, the demonstrators disbanded <u>quickly</u>.
- (A) adjective
- (B) noun
- (C) preposition
- (D) none of the above

44. The scholarship money went <u>toward</u> his college fund.
- (A) adjective
- (B) noun
- (C) preposition
- (D) none of the above

45. The <u>retractable</u> wheels on the plane got stuck.
- (A) adjective
- (B) noun
- (C) preposition
- (D) none of the above

Step 4: Grammar and Usage
Section 1—Grammar Part B

> Read the sentence below. Decide if the underlined word is a helping verb, linking verb, or action verb. Fill in the bubble for your answer.
>
> **Sample:** The football game <u>lasted</u> three hours.
> - Ⓐ helping verb
> - Ⓑ linking verb
> - Ⓒ action verb

Directions: Read each sentence below. Decide if each underlined word is a helping verb, linking verb, or action verb. Fill in the bubble for your answer.

46. The Frank family <u>lived</u> in hiding for four long years.
    - Ⓐ helping verb
    - Ⓑ linking verb
    - Ⓒ action verb

47. The marching band <u>was</u> playing during the halftime entertainment.
    - Ⓐ helping verb
    - Ⓑ linking verb
    - Ⓒ action verb

48. Martin Luther King, Jr. <u>is</u> an inspiration to everyone.
    - Ⓐ helping verb
    - Ⓑ linking verb
    - Ⓒ action verb

49. Next week, the championship trophy <u>will</u> be at school.
    - Ⓐ helping verb
    - Ⓑ linking verb
    - Ⓒ action verb

50. Thousands of students <u>took</u> the final exam.
    - Ⓐ helping verb
    - Ⓑ linking verb
    - Ⓒ action verb

Summative Test

Step 4: Grammar and Usage
Section 2—Usage

> Read the sentences below. The area that may contain an error is underlined in each sentence. Select the one with the correct placement of commas. Fill in the bubble for your answer.
>
> **Sample:**
>   Ⓐ The player packed <u>his helmet pads, and mouthpiece.</u>
>   Ⓑ The player packed <u>his helmet, pads, and mouthpiece.</u>
>   Ⓒ The player packed <u>his helmet, pads and mouthpiece.</u>
>   Ⓓ None is correct.

Directions: Read the sentences below. The area that may contain an error is underlined in each sentence. Select the one with the correct placement of commas. Fill in the bubble for your answer.

51.   Ⓐ The athlete played <u>lacrosse, football, soccer and basketball.</u>
     Ⓑ The athlete played <u>lacrosse football, soccer and basketball.</u>
     Ⓒ The athlete played <u>lacrosse, football, soccer, and basketball.</u>
     Ⓓ None is correct.

52.   Ⓐ My sister has moved to <u>200 High Street, Lowville Rhode Island 44411.</u>
     Ⓑ My sister has moved to <u>200 High Street, Lowville, Rhode Island 44411.</u>
     Ⓒ My sister has moved to <u>200 High Street Lowville, Rhode Island 44411.</u>
     Ⓓ None is correct.

53.   Ⓐ The Declaration of <u>Independence was signed on July 4, 1776.</u>
     Ⓑ The Declaration of <u>Independence was signed on July 4 1776.</u>
     Ⓒ The Declaration of <u>Independence, was signed on July 4, 1776.</u>
     Ⓓ None is correct.

54.   Ⓐ "The girl in the red <u>car," whispered Tom "is the new band leader."</u>
     Ⓑ "The girl in the red <u>car," whispered Tom "is the new band, leader."</u>
     Ⓒ "The girl in the red <u>car," whispered, Tom "is the new band leader."</u>
     Ⓓ None is correct.

55.   Ⓐ On April 14, 1775, Paul Revere <u>rode out of Boston, warned the minutemen and earned a place in history.</u>
     Ⓑ On April 14, 1775, Paul Revere <u>rode out of Boston, warned the minutemen, and earned a place in history.</u>
     Ⓒ On April 14, 1775, Paul Revere <u>rode out of Boston warned the minutemen and earned a place in history.</u>
     Ⓓ None is correct.

Summative Test

Step 4: Grammar and Usage
Section 3—Sentence Structure Part A

Read the sentence below. Decide if the underlined word is a predicate nominative, a predicate adjective, a direct object, or none of the above. Fill in the bubble for your answer.

Sample: The coach carried a large <u>notebook</u>.
- Ⓐ predicate nominative
- Ⓑ predicate adjective
- Ⓒ direct object
- Ⓓ none of the above

Directions: Read each sentence below. Decide if the underlined word is a predicate nominative, a predicate adjective, a direct object, or none of the above. Fill in the bubble for your answer.

56. Millions of people heard Dr. King's <u>speech</u>.
- Ⓐ predicate nominative
- Ⓑ predicate adjective
- Ⓒ direct object
- Ⓓ none of the above

57. The speech is <u>famous</u> all around the world.
- Ⓐ predicate nominative
- Ⓑ predicate adjective
- Ⓒ direct object
- Ⓓ none of the above

58. Mt. St. Helens is an active <u>volcano</u>.
- Ⓐ predicate nominative
- Ⓑ predicate adjective
- Ⓒ direct object
- Ⓓ none of the above

59. The <u>class</u> visited the new exhibit at the art museum.
- Ⓐ predicate nominative
- Ⓑ predicate adjective
- Ⓒ direct object
- Ⓓ none of the above

60. The basketball player was extremely <u>tall</u>.
- Ⓐ predicate nominative
- Ⓑ predicate adjective
- Ⓒ direct object
- Ⓓ none of the above

Summative Test

Step 4: Grammar and Usage
Section 3—Sentence Structure Part B

> **Sample:** Read the two sentences. Underline the **direct object** in each sentence. Write a **compound direct object** sentence using one of these conjunctions: **and**, **but**, **or**. Underline the conjunction used in the sentence.
>
> The student studied <u>math</u>. The student studied history.
>
> _____

61. Read the two sentences. Underline the **predicate nominative** in each sentence. Write a **compound predicate nominative** sentence using one of these conjunctions: **and**, **but**, **or**. Underline the conjunction used in the sentence.

    Martin Luther King, Jr. was a minister. Martin Luther King, Jr. was a preacher.

    _____

62. Read the two sentences. Underline the **predicate adjective** in each sentence. Write a **compound predicate adjective** sentence using one of these conjunctions: **and**, **but**, **or**. Underline the conjunction used in the sentence.

    The puzzle was large. The puzzle was not difficult.

    _____

63. Read the two sentences. Underline the **direct object** in each sentence. Write a **compound direct object** sentence using one of these conjunctions: **and**, **but**, **or**. Underline the conjunction used in the sentence.

    The old car had a new fender. The old car had new headlights.

    _____

64. Read the two sentences. Underline the **predicate nominative** in each sentence. Write a **compound predicate nominative** sentence using one of these conjunctions: **and**, **but**, **or**. Underline the conjunction used in the sentence.

    Mr. T. Brown was the math teacher. Mr. T. Brown was the assistant football coach.

    _____

65. Read the two sentences. Underline the **predicate nominative** in each sentence. Write a **compound predicate nominative** using one of these conjunctions: **and**, **but**, **or**. Underline the conjunction used in the sentence.

    Your one prize could be a car. Your one prize could be a bike.

    _____

Step 6: Speaking and Writing

In Book D, you have been learning how to identify and describe character traits. Use what you have learned to complete this composition. Read the directions carefully. Make sure you complete all of the requirements described below.

Directions: Composition Assignment

Write about a person you admire greatly. This can be someone you know personally or someone you have read about. Explain in detail the particular traits that make this person special.

Your writing will be scored on how well you:
- **Relate information about the person you describe.**
- **Organize your writing with a strong introduction, supporting ideas, and a conclusion.**
- **Use details to describe the person.**
- **Use correct grammar, spelling, punctuation, and capitalization.**

Progress Indicators

Test of Silent Word Reading Fluency—Form A

Record of Scores

Student Responses

Example 1   in yes go me see

Example 2   ofgoliketwobig/
onheupyesget/

When your teacher says to begin, turn the page and start the test.

onatgetruncarisfunbluebiglikeback/
eachmuchthreezooapplefarflywould/
wayunderbirdfoundegglunchyardlive/
staygirlcakeofbutpetroomlightvery/
pulldayiceoldeightlargewolfkeyfix/
straightwildgrewaboveswimtrouble/
setdrivequickkickrollbottlejollysky/
fewdesertfaultgazepressrootcrept/
leakjudgehoundtightbuiltcoachfresh/
breezebulbawfulmountelvesbirthwake/
swungmoundrentguestgullbulgenurse/
saucequiltnavymurmurzerogravykettle/
tigercouncilfolktuckplumjunglerhythm/
limblilyrovemothlungfueldazzlemercy/
symbolboltclenchbluffhullgermthrive/
neglectnudgefleshlurchvarietylaurel/
drenchpulsegriefyachtquizstaffcycle/
emberbulkquarrycounseljurypeltfilm/
strictdepthmuzzlefudgeficklefilter/
lureutterbluntvaryreekgaugeutilize/
jeernymphgiltpoachwieldprivacyfrenzy/
molarlynchracialaccessgildjauntsurly/
ebbdivulgegaietystaunchcliqueevolve/
envoydirgedelvebaublenaiveductvigil/
girthfoiblefeignauravoguetautdefer/
fetterlewdlenientcysthulkdetervie/
wreakcommunalduresspreceptelixir/
sullysecular girddubcoerceguile/
epochprecludepulsarvernacularquaff/
symposiumrazeimbuejunctureneophyte/
encomiumfecundacquiescejocund/
egressimbrogliocajolepecuniaryfacile/

Form A

DRP Reading Test

Directions to Student

This is a test to find out how well you read. The test contains passages for you to read. Words are missing from the passages. Wherever a word is missing, there is a blank line with a number on it. Next to the passage, you will find the same number and five words. Choose the word that makes the best sense in the blank.

Next to the word, fill in the bubble for the answer you have chosen.

Read Sample **S-1** below and see how the right answer has been marked in your booklet. Then read Sample **S-2** and fill in the bubble next to the correct answer.

Record of Scores

Samples

It was sunny and hot for days.
Then the ___S–1___ changed. It turned
cloudy and cool.

S–1 Ⓐ price Ⓑ road
Ⓒ job ● weather
Ⓔ size

It isn't safe to go out today. There
was too much ___S–2___ yesterday.
Many streets are flooded with water.

S–2 Ⓐ rain Ⓑ food
Ⓒ mail Ⓓ noise
Ⓔ work

Look at the answer for Sample **S-1**. The letter **D** is filled in because the word **weather** makes the best sense in the blank.

For Sample **S-2**, you should have filled in the bubble for the letter **A** because the word **rain** makes the best sense in the blank.

As you can see, you may not be sure of the answer until you have read the sentences that come after the blank. So be sure to read enough to choose your answer.

DRP Reading Test

You are not expected to read at the same speed as other students or to answer the same number of items. As you work on this test, you will find that the passages become harder to read. Do your best to read as many passages as you can and to answer as many items as you can. Work carefully and do not rush. You will be given as much time as you need.

Remember, mark only one answer for each item. If you want to change an answer, be sure to erase or cross out your first mark. Then mark the answer you want.

Only female spiders spin webs. A female spider uses her web to trap food and as her home. The female spider makes her web out of fine silk threads. Silk, a kind of protein, is made by glands inside the female spider's body. The spider secretes the silk threads and connects them together to make her web. Making a web takes a lot of time and energy. Much __1__ is needed.

Flying insects are caught in spider webs because they cannot see the delicate threads. The threads are too __2__. The insects remain trapped because most threads are coated with droplets of glue. The spider's glue-making gland coats the thread as she secretes it. The spider makes a few threads without glue and weaves these throughout her web. She travels freely around her web on these dry threads. They do not __3__ her. The center of the web, where the spider often sits, is made of dry threads.

A female spider knows that an insect is caught in her web because she feels the threads vibrate as the insect struggles to free itself. Its __4__ alerts the spider. She feels the vibrations with her legs. The spider must hurry to bind the trapped insect before it escapes. She must not __5__. The spider bites the insect several times, injecting it with poison. This poison paralyzes and kills the insect. The spider then turns the dead insect round and round with her legs, wrapping it in more silk thread. If she is not hungry at that time, she stores her catch, hanging it from the web by a short silk thread. She will __6__ the insect later.

A spider also weaves bits of leaves into one edge of her web. This area offers her protection. She may retreat here at night or in bad weather. She has __7__ when she needs it.

1 Ⓐ labor Ⓑ water
  Ⓒ support Ⓓ soil
     Ⓔ light

2 Ⓐ long Ⓑ thin
  Ⓒ smooth Ⓓ flat
     Ⓔ numerous

3 Ⓐ burn Ⓑ warn
  Ⓒ hide Ⓓ stop
     Ⓔ interest

4 Ⓐ shape Ⓑ smell
  Ⓒ taste Ⓓ sound
     Ⓔ movement

5 Ⓐ delay Ⓑ change
  Ⓒ yield Ⓓ jump
     Ⓔ approach

6 Ⓐ help Ⓑ secure
  Ⓒ eat Ⓓ fight
     Ⓔ murder

7 Ⓐ speed Ⓑ meat
  Ⓒ shelter Ⓓ strength
     Ⓔ exercise

(Go to the Next Page)

Mosses are small green plants that grow almost everywhere on earth. One of the most useful kinds is sphagnum or peat moss. This type of moss is found in ponds, on lake shores, and in swampy areas. All of these __8__ are damp. Peat moss thrives in the presence of water, often growing right in it.

Sphagnum is frequently found growing like a mat on the surface of a pond. As the moss develops, it advances farther and farther across the pond. The mat keeps __9__. Soon, it blankets much of the surface. Older parts of the plants die below the water line, and vegetable matter washes in among the decaying stems. Eventually, the moss mat is several feet thick. As it gets heavier, the mat begins to sink. However, it __10__ slowly. It drops so gradually that new growth continues above the surface.

After many years, the dead plant bodies become so tightly pressed together they can be sliced into blocks. In some regions of the world, the dried blocks are burned as fuel. This gives people __11__ that they need. The blocks are used not only for warming homes but also for cooking.

Sphagnum has other uses. Like a sponge, it soaks up many times its weight in water. For this reason, nurseries wrap sphagnum around the roots of plants. This __12__ protects the plants. The layer keeps the roots damp until planting time. Peat moss is also used by gardeners, who mix it into poor soil. The peat moss improves the soil and helps it retain moisture. That is why gardeners __13__ the moss.

Because sphagnum is so absorbent, it has been used for bandages and surgical dressings. Sphagnum also happens to be mildly antiseptic. This makes it doubly valuable for use on __14__. For many years, American Indians used sphagnum to make a salve for treating cuts, and the British put it on sores to help them heal.

8   Ⓐ rocks   Ⓑ leaves
     Ⓒ months   Ⓓ seeds
       Ⓔ places

9   Ⓐ spreading   Ⓑ breaking
     Ⓒ tipping   Ⓓ smelling
       Ⓔ yellowing

10 Ⓐ cools   Ⓑ flowers
     Ⓒ ages   Ⓓ falls
       Ⓔ separates

11 Ⓐ clothing   Ⓑ heat
     Ⓒ work   Ⓓ money
       Ⓔ room

12 Ⓐ covering   Ⓑ fence
     Ⓒ cleaning   Ⓓ stream
       Ⓔ temperature

13 Ⓐ air   Ⓑ add
     Ⓒ store   Ⓓ test
       Ⓔ move

14 Ⓐ stones   Ⓑ paths
     Ⓒ wounds   Ⓓ tables
       Ⓔ roofs

PTM–204–1.2
Form CD–2

(Go to the Next Page)

Dyes have been used to color cloth for thousands of years. Among ancient dyes, none was more highly valued than the Tyrian, or "royal," purple of the Phoenicians. This dye was considered very desirable because its color was exceptionally rich. It was also __15__ for a second reason. Unlike other dyes, which faded, Tyrian purple was colorfast and retained its deep crimson hue.

15 Ⓐ cooled   Ⓑ strained
    Ⓒ prized   Ⓓ changed
      Ⓔ removed

Tyrian purple was extracted from murex and purpura snails, types of shellfish found in the Mediterranean. Making even the smallest amount of the dye required a great many snails. Divers had to go below again and again to gather enough for processing. The __16__ needed was enormous. It is estimated that it took 336,000 snails to make one ounce of dye.

16 Ⓐ number   Ⓑ speed
    Ⓒ heat   Ⓓ area
      Ⓔ control

Because of all the work involved in making Tyrian purple dye, it was very expensive. Tyrian purple cloth cost so much that only royalty and the wealthy could afford it. Other __17__ could not. In time, the wearing of purple garments was limited to certain classes of officials, and purple became an imperial color. Competing merchants tried to make a Tyrian-like purple, at much lower cost, by mixing red and blue vegetable dyes. But they could not __18__ the Tyrian purple. The vegetable dyes never had the brilliance of the snail-based dye.

17 Ⓐ ships   Ⓑ routes
    Ⓒ designs   Ⓓ people
      Ⓔ materials

18 Ⓐ store   Ⓑ hide
    Ⓒ match   Ⓓ buy
      Ⓔ recognized

The seafaring Phoenicians searched the Mediterranean for dye-giving snails, and found large quantities along the Asia Minor coast. Similar __19__ were made elsewhere. In Greece and North Africa and wherever else they found the shellfish, the Phoenicians built dye shops. Shops producing Tyrian purple were thus not confined to the city of Tyre itself. Rather, the shops were __20__. They dotted the shore all the way to Spain, thousands of miles away. The Phoenicians did not manufacture all this purple dye just for their own use. The dye was __21__. Merchants exported it throughout the world, and made fortunes in this commerce.

19 Ⓐ styles   Ⓑ sales
    Ⓒ treaties   Ⓓ mistakes
      Ⓔ discoveries

20 Ⓐ bare   Ⓑ dark
    Ⓒ small   Ⓓ armed
      Ⓔ scattered

21 Ⓐ wasted   Ⓑ traded
    Ⓒ warmed   Ⓓ poured
      Ⓔ stirred

(Go to the Next Page)

During the Middle Ages, tapestries were an integral part of the life of European aristocracy. These beautiful fabric pictures, which were used rather like wallpaper, became popular in part because of their portability. Nobles traveled about their lands almost all year, and their tapestries could be rolled up and taken along. They were easy to __22__. Tapestries not only enabled the bleak stone walls of each castle along the route to come alive with color and pattern, but also blocked cold drafts. Thus, __23__ was increased.

Responsibilities for a noble's tapestries belonged to one servant, who was in charge of the many workers needed for transportation, storage, and care. Since the collection was valuable, there were guards among the workers. The tapestries had to be __24__. Otherwise, they might be stolen.

The servant in charge also decided which pieces to hang at each castle. The tapestries had to look right together as well as cover the walls. Good __25__ was required. So was the ability to make do, since tapestries were often made only in general sizes—small, medium, and large. Because these sizes did not exactly match castle walls, the servant mixed and matched different pieces. If they were too wide for a wall, the tapesties were often bent around the corner. If they were too long, they were bunched up at the bottom. Tapestries are, of course, easy to __26__. Like other textiles, they are flexible. However, there were times when tapestries were cut to fit the size of a given room. Many were __27__ in this way.

The walls of each castle were always ready for tapestries: there were hooks in place at all times. The hooks were installed by the thousands. Such large __28__ are easy to understand. The weight of the wall hangings required a great deal of support. Permanent hooks also allowed tapestries to be changed quickly to suit their owner's mood or to mark a great event.

22 Ⓐ move   Ⓑ fix
   Ⓒ buy   Ⓓ clean
   Ⓔ manufacture

23 Ⓐ wealth   Ⓑ comfort
   Ⓒ light   Ⓓ clothing
   Ⓔ authority

24 Ⓐ balanced   Ⓑ watched
   Ⓒ connected   Ⓓ accepted
   Ⓔ completed

25 Ⓐ aim   Ⓑ wool
   Ⓒ speed   Ⓓ taste
   Ⓔ weather

26 Ⓐ brush   Ⓑ obtain
   Ⓒ fold   Ⓓ design
   Ⓔ copy

27 Ⓐ ruined   Ⓑ chosen
   Ⓒ stretched   Ⓓ soiled
   Ⓔ located

28 Ⓐ halls   Ⓑ wagons
   Ⓒ borders   Ⓓ windows
   Ⓔ numbers

TAP–341–2.2
Form CD–2

(Go to the Next Page)

Wavelengths of light from red to violet are detected by the human eye. These visible wavelengths, averaging about 55 millionths of a centimeter, do not reflect the full electromagnetic spectrum. Only a __29__ is seen.

Snakes, like humans, see light in the red to violet range. Unlike humans, however, many snakes have the additional capacity to detect infrared light. Infrared light waves represent heat. This means that the __30__ must be warm. Living creatures with high body temperatures emit strong infrared waves. Such creatures make up the major part of most snakes' diets. Therefore, a snake's ability to "see" infrared rays serves a vital purpose. It helps the snake recognize __31__. Snakes often prey on small mammals, which have relatively high body temperatures.

The snake's infrared vision depends upon its "pit organs," circular cavities sunk deep into the head of the snake. These __32__ are always found in pairs. A snakes's head may have up to twenty-six such indentations. Each pit is lined with thousands of nerve endings that respond to infrared light. These structures __33__ heat. When heat (in the form of infrared rays) strikes a pit organ, nerve impulses are transmitted to the snake's brain.

In the brain, impulses from the various pit organs are analyzed. Comparing the strength of the impulses reveals the exact direction from which the heat emanates. This process is quite precise. Even small animals can be __34__ Ordinarily, the snake's normal vision supplements its infrared vision as a tool for finding prey. In one experiment, however, scientists blindfolded a rattlesnake so that only its pit organs were exposed. A hot iron was then placed some distance away. When prodded by an experimenter, the snake lunged at the smoldering iron. It was no suprise that the snake __35__. What was suprising was the accuracy of the strike. Guided only by infrared rays, the snake typically landed within five degrees of its target.

29 (A) mark   (B) figure
   (C) portion   (D) hole
     (E) pattern

30 (A) rain   (B) nest
   (C) stone   (D) source
     (E) afternoon

31 (A) sand   (B) food
   (C) shelter   (D) wood
     (E) water

32 (A) bones   (B) plants
   (C) eggs   (D) rocks
     (E) hollows

33 (A) sense   (B) lose
   (C) avoid   (D) spread
     (E) exchange

34 (A) controlled (B) located
   (C) burned   (D) removed
     (E) protected

35 (A) rested   (B) grew
   (C) looked   (D) rolled
     (E) attacked

(Stop)

Progress Indicators

Spelling Inventory

Record of Scores

Student Responses

Write the words that your teacher dictates.

1. _____
2. _____
3. _____
4. _____
5. _____
6. _____
7. _____
8. _____
9. _____
10. _____
11. _____
12. _____
13. _____
14. _____
15. _____

16. _____
17. _____
18. _____
19. _____
20. _____
21. _____
22. _____
23. _____
24. _____
25. _____
26. _____
27. _____
28. _____
29. _____
30. _____